¿Qué hace el CONSERJE?

What Does a JANITOR Do?

Rita Kidde
Traducido por Eida de la Vega

PowerKiDS press™

New York

Published in 2015 by The Rosen Publishing Group, Inc.
29 East 21st Street, New York, NY 10010

First Edition

Editor: Amelie von Zumbusch
Book Design: Colleen Bialecki
Photo Research: Katie Stryker

Spanish translation: Eida de la Vega

Photo Credits: Cover Dirk Ott/iStock/Thinkstock; p. 5 Blend Images- ERproductions Ltd/Brand X Pictures/Getty Images; p. 6 Lucarelli Temistocle/Shutterstock.com; p. 9 Fuse/Getty Images; p. 10 Muntz/The Image Bank/Getty Images; p. 13 Daniel Lai/ Aurora/Getty Images; p. 14 Valerie Loiseleux/E+/Getty Images; p. 17 Justin Geoffrey/Iconica/Getty Images; p. 18 Vadim Ratnikov/Shutterstock.com; p. 21 Globalphotogroup/Shutterstock.com; p. 22 SW Productions/Stockbyte/Getty Images.

Library of Congress Cataloging-in-Publication Data

Kidde, Rita.
 What does a janitor do? = ¿Qué hace el conserje? / by Rita Kidde ; translated by Eida de la Vega.
    pages cm. — (Jobs in my school = Oficios en mi escuela)
 Text in English and Spanish.
 Includes index.
 ISBN 978-1-4777-6791-7 (library binding)
 1. School custodians—Juvenile literature. I. Title. II. Title: ¿Qué hace el conserje?
 LB3235.K57 2015
 371.6'8—dc23
                       2013047589

Websites: Due to the changing nature of Internet links, PowerKids Press has developed an online list of websites related to the subject of this book. This site is updated regularly. Please use this link to access the list: www.powerkidslinks.com/josc/jani/

CONTENIDO

CONTENTS

Los **conserjes** de la escuela tienen un trabajo importante. Mantienen limpia la escuela.

School **janitors** have big jobs. They keep schools clean.

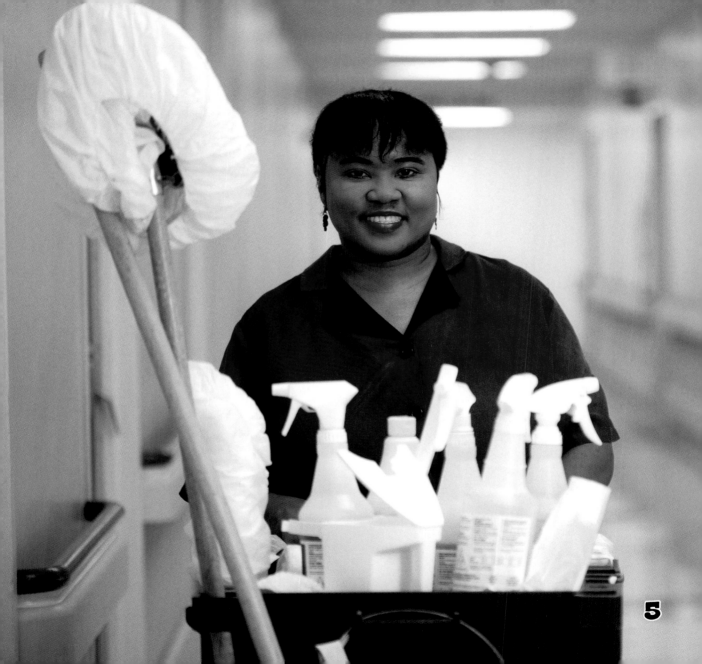

Cuando algo se rompe, lo arreglan. Reponen los suministros que se acaban.

They fix things when they break. They replace supplies, too.

En algunas escuelas
se les llama custodios.

At some schools, they are
called custodians.

Los conserjes limpian
el suelo y las ventanas.

Janitors clean floors. They
clean windows.

Hacen la mayoría de su trabajo por la noche. Así, nadie los interrumpe cuando limpian.

They do most of their work at night. That way, no one gets in the way when they are cleaning.

¿Alguna vez has subido tu silla al pupitre? Eso ayuda a los conserjes para que puedan limpiar el suelo.

Have you ever put your chair up on your desk? Doing this makes it easier for janitors to clean the floors.

Los conserjes sacan
la **basura**. Cada año,
en los Estados Unidos se tira
cerca de 200 millones
de toneladas (181 millones t)
de basura.

Janitors take out **trash**. Each
year, Americans make about
200 million tons (181 million t)
of trash!

17

En climas fríos, los conserjes palean nieve. Alaska es el estado donde más nieve cae en los Estados Unidos.

In cold weather, janitors shovel snow. Alaska gets the most snow of any US state.

Los conserjes mantienen las **calderas** en funcionamiento. Estas calientan las escuelas.

They keep the **furnaces** going. These heat schools.

21

Sé siempre amable con
los conserjes. ¡Sin ellos,
la escuela sería un desastre!

_____

Always be nice to janitors.
The school would be a mess
without them!

PALABRAS QUE DEBES SABER
WORDS TO KNOW

(la) caldera
furnace

(la) conserje
janitor

(la) basura
trash

ÍNDICE

INDEX